Frank Sewall

An Essay on the Spiritual Nature of Force

Frank Sewall

An Essay on the Spiritual Nature of Force

ISBN/EAN: 9783337334444

Printed in Europe, USA, Canada, Australia, Japan

Cover: Foto ©Lupo / pixelio.de

More available books at **www.hansebooks.com**

URBANA UNIVERSITY.

——————

AN ESSAY

ON THE

Spiritual Nature of Force

BY

THOS. FREEMAN MOSES, A. M., M. D.,

Prof. of Natural Science in Urbana University.

READ AT THE ANNUAL COMMENCEMENT, JUNE 7, 1871.

TOGETHER WITH THE

Inaugural Address of the President,

TO WHICH IS ADDED THE

Catalogue and Prospectus of the University

For the Present Year.

——————

CINCINNATI:

ROBERT CLARKE & CO.

1871.

AN ESSAY

ON THE

SPIRITUAL NATURE OF FORCE

BY

THOMAS F. MOSES, A. M., M. D.,

Professor of Natural Science in Urbana University,

URBANA, OHIO.

On the Spiritual Nature of Force.

Swedenborg, in his treatise upon the Divine Love and Wisdom, says: "For the dead to act upon the living, or, what is the same thing, for the natural to act upon the spiritual, is entirely contrary to order; and to think it possible, is opposed to the light of sound reason." A knowledge, then, of the true order of nature is necessary to the exercise of sound reason. If we examine the past history of philosophy, we find it to be a controversy for the supremacy on the part of spirit and matter. "I will believe only what I see," says the materialist, and he strengthens his eyes with powerful lenses, and hopes to discover the secrets of nature and the origin of things by such aids to his natural senses. "I will see only what I believe," is, on the other hand, the motto of the spiritualist; and, since the days of Galileo, he has ever regarded with distrust the inventions and discoveries of science. The time has happily arrived when this mutual distrust may cease, and the advocates of the respective agencies of spirit and matter in the origin and continuance of things may henceforth work hand in hand in the great search after truth.

We are entering upon a new era, an era in which the facts of science no longer clash with the truths of revelation. Science has been regenerated, for the contrast between its present and former condition is not so much the result of a progress in the old paths as a veritable new birth. The startling fact of the unity of all the forces operating in nature is a discovery in won-

derful harmony with the Divine Unity and Personality. On the
other hand, it shall no longer be deemed unscientific to acknowl-
edge a supernatural First Cause. Thus, how to bridge over the
great gulf, which till now has apparently existed between science
and revelation, is a problem which to day admits of solution. Not
that in the minds of right-thinking men any such separation has
had real existence, but by those whose patient and persevering
labor has heaped up the treasures of science, and who guard them
with a jealous care, a connected succession of causes is demanded,
and justly so. This can not be found in any system of theology
other than that of the New Church. Let us not hastily accuse
them of infidelity. For want of a proper starting point, they are
mistaken in their deductions; but they are doubtless honest in
their convictions, and we must confess that a large portion of
scientific discovery is due to their efforts. We believe, however,
that no fact is more clearly proven, or more solidly established,
than that the first cause of all things is supernatural and constantly active, and upon this postulate all true science must be
based.

Let us review briefly the modern aspect of the physical sciences,
with especial reference to this new doctrine of force. We shall
endeavor to show, or at least to make it probable, that this force
can not, in any instance, originate in matter itself, but must have
a spiritual origin. With this end in view, it will be necessary to
examine somewhat in detail the brilliant and plausible theories
now held and propagated by some of the most eminent scientists
of the day, to show, if possible, wherein they are fallacious. And,
first, what is the present aspect of the physical sciences?

Under the names of heat, light, electricity, magnetism, galvan-
ism, chemical affinity, and gravity, have been designated most of
the activities of matter. All these were believed to be elementary
principles, with distinct characteristics and properties. In the
progress of science, however, a more and more intimate connection was found to exist between these various forces. The molecular attractions known as chemical affinity were seen to have a
striking analogy with the mutual attractions of the great plan-

etary masses of the universe. Heat and light were observed to accompany many of the manifestations of chemical affinity, as well as of electricity and magnetism, especially when the motion of these forces, while in operation, was interrupted. More recently, the exact equivalence of heat and mechanical force, and their mutual convertibility, have been demonstrated. Thus, in the minds of many, a new conception of nature, founded upon these mutual relations, has been struggling into existence. This conception has finally had birth in the wonderful discovery of the unity of all the physical forces, which, like the dawn of a new revelation, has poured a flood of light into every department of scientific investigation, grouping together in an harmonious manner all known facts, arranging and co-ordinating them, and rapidly assigning to each new discovery its relative value and appropriate station. In all the history of science, we shall find no theory so grand, so well supported by facts, and of so universal application; and as such, we may regard it as the fitting sequence of that grander revelation of spiritual truths which we of the new theology hold. Upon its broad basis is destined to rise a new system of science, which will always be in perfect accord with divine revelation; and religion may fearlessly welcome each new scientific discovery, not as a possible weapon to be directed against herself, but as a fresh bulwark of defense against the powers of evil.

There are no longer *forces*, then, in the sense of independent natural agencies, but there is a force or energy which flows down into matter, manifesting itself as heat, light, chemical affinity, and in other ways, according to the various uses it has to serve in the material world. All these may be said to be modes of motion, and motion is the sensible operation of force. This force does not reside in matter, does not belong to matter, but is above matter and nature—is in its essence supernatural or spiritual. And here the questions may be asked: what is matter, and what is spirit, and how are they able to operate, the one upon the other?

I am aware that no end of fruitless speculation has been expended upon these and kindred topics, and I would by all means avoid the metaphysical maze which so-called philosophers have woven out of the mists of their own self-consciousness. Without attempting to describe what spirit and matter are in their essence —a task manifestly impossible—we content ourselves with indicating a few of the characteristic properties of each, which correspond to that distinct discrimination made between them by every human mind.

It is reasonable to assume that matter, in its elementary form, is simple and homogeneous, and that in the beginning it was equally diffused throughout the universe. To this elementary form of matter, modern science has given the name of ether; and it is the different aggregation of the atoms of ether that enter into the composition of the elementary particles of simple bodies, such as iron, carbon, oxygen, etc. That is to say, to use the language of the author of La Physique Moderne, "the molecules of these bodies do not differ in their substance, but simply in the interior arrangement of the etherial atoms which compose them." Some of the well-known properties of matter are extension, impenetrability, and inertia. From matter we get the notion of space and time, which are peculiar to it. When we say that matter is diffused throughout space, we must not infer that it is infinite, in any proper sense of that term. Indefinite extension is not infinity. Matter is finite, and always remains the same in kind, however indefinitely extended. Throughout the whole extent of matter, we may further assume that a state of equilibrium at first existed. Now, is there anything in the nature of matter itself which should disturb this equilibrium? Certainly not. Inertia, or the disposition which matter has to remain at rest until set in motion by some force outside of itself, is one of the properties of matter. This principle of inertia "lies at the very basis of all mechanics, and is directly demonstrated by all human experience." Over this chaos the Spirit of God must have moved to originate the first motion.

Now, spirit is that which flows into matter and gives it activity or motion. It is energy, actual and potential. In other words, it is the force by which matter is set in motion, and which is the cause of its various transformations. It is invisible, imponderable, can not be handled. It is the indwelling essence that gives to matter its definite shapes, and fits it for its various uses. Spirit is the cause—the forms of matter are the effect. We acquire a knowledge of matter by touch, sight, smell, in general by our bodily senses. The nature of spirit is known rather by the tests applied by our reason, than from the evidence of our senses. Its presence in nature is universal, and its operation constant. Remove its influence, and chaos would reign once more. The relation existing between spirit and matter is that of a true correspondence, like that existing between the soul and body of man. In support of these statements, we make use, in a purely scientific point of view, of the following illustration :

It is now generally conceded that from the sun of our planetary system proceed all those activities of matter operating in that system which we know by the name of the physical forces. We are all familiar with the recent results obtained from observing the appearance of the sun during a total eclipse. These observations have been made in the most careful manner and with the most delicate instruments known to science. The result of them is to give additional proof of the common nature of the auroral and electrical phenomena exhibited in our own atmosphere with like phenomena displayed by the sun's corona, rendering it probable that they have one and the same origin. In like manner it is well nigh demonstrated that the spots on the sun have an intimate connection with those wonderful columns seen to project from its sphere during the totality of an eclipse, millions of miles into space, like living fountains of light and heat. These spots and protuberances have a direct influence upon the auroral and magnetic phenomena of our earth, and also upon its changes of climate and its animal and vegetable life. The spectroscope has shown us that in the sun's atmosphere exist, in their most subtle form, many, if not all the materials composing our earth and other earths. Here they exist in their purity and essence, and here is effected their conjunction with spiritual forces. Is it not, perhaps, this unceasing commingling of spirit with matter which enables the sun to give out its exhaustless stores of light and heat, which are the first forms of material force or motion? The most minute investigations conducted by scientific men have not been able to discover any sensible diminution in the sun's heat within known periods of time. It is said to be *self-luminous* also, an acknowledgment that its light has no known material source of supply. The materialist will here bring forward his doctrine of the conservation of force, but it is a fallacy to suppose that this conservation of force completes its circle in nature. In the exact ratio in which these physical forces, after being derived from the sun, are converted into each other, Nature displays a characteristic economy; but that they are able to restore an equivalent to the sun, their source, is a supposition, not only unnecessary, but entirely unsupported by a single fact.

Let us ascend the scale of matter and note the operation of spiritual causes in the organized forms of the animal and vegetable kingdoms. The author of that fascinating essay, the Physical Basis of Life, describes in a clear and striking manner the structural element which enters into the composition of all plants and living beings, from man to the lowest cell-germ of vegetable life. While science is indebted to him for a concise and lucid statement of the order of nature in the employment of a simple, fundamental substance for the exhibition of the phenomena of life, we are far from accepting his conclusions as to the functions of this basis of life. The statement of Prof. Huxley's theory runs, briefly, thus: A unity of faculty, form, and structure pervades the whole living world. A substance known to physiologists as protoplasm is the physical or material basis for the exhibition of all the phenomena of life in man and plant. Man, whale, fungus, and microscopic animalcule enjoy an identity of structure, and, with the exception of a difference of degree, all possess like powers and faculties. These powers, faculties, and activities, exhibited in the single protoplasmic cell as a mere vibration of its walls, make the creature which lies at the bottom of the animal scale; when variously diversified to correspond to that complexity of parts and functions belonging to the highest animal known in the scale, and accompanied with manifestations of intellect, feeling, and will, we have *man*. As regards plants, in respect of form they are not separable from animals, and, in many cases, "it is a mere matter of convention whether we call an organism an animal or a plant." An important difference, however, between them is that plants can manufacture protoplasm out of the mineral kingdom, which the animal can not do. The latter depends for its supply upon the plant. Thus, ordinary matter, as it exists in the animal kingdom under the forms of carbon, hydrogen, oxygen, and nitrogen, becomes, successively, plant, animal, and man.

In the onward march of this theory in the construction of man out of matter, several important points are conceded by the way. The mineral never becomes the plant without the intervention of pre-existing protoplasm to act as the fulcrum for elevating the dead into living matter. The plant, in its turn, can not live upon the separate elements out of which its tissue is formed. They must first be variously combined. Its existence depends upon the pre-existence of certain compounds, those of carbonic acid, water, and ammonia. Again, "an animal can not make protoplasm, but must take it ready made from some other animal or plant." Thus, the protoplasm of the animal has the same relation to that of the plant as the protoplasm of the plant has to that of the mineral compounds from which it grows. Here we have a clear interruption at two points in this development theory, and these are at the place of transition of the mineral into the plant, and of the plant into the animal. Yes, there are insuperable barriers separating the three great kingdoms of nature, and no one of them may ever pass over its prescribed limits into another. Behold, how short a distance the science which recognizes only the agency of matter leads us in the solution of the problem of life, and witness, from the following general conclusion, how far it may conduct us into error! The author of this theory, so true in the main in point of fact, so erroneous in doctrine, frankly confesses that he finds no logical halting-place between the admission of the identical structure of all living forms and the further conclusion that all vital action may be said to be the result of the molecular forces of the protoplasm which displays it; and, finally, that his thoughts and our thoughts are but the expression of the molecular changes in that matter of life which is the source of our other vital phenomena. Furthermore, although volition is admitted to have some influence over the course of events, yet anything like spontaneity of action is totally denied. By this is meant that any given phenomenon must be the effect of a material cause. A spontaneous act has, indeed, no material cause, but it is unwarrantable logic to assert that it can have no cause whatever, and, consequently, that no act can be spontaneous. The act appears *spontaneous* from the very fact of its independence of all natural causes. But man is not a mere automaton, containing within himself all the springs of his life and his actions, nor can he be the sole cause of his own experiences. It is necessary to admit the influence and operation of spiritual causes.

We have thus far tacitly admitted the truth of the theory of the identity of the basis of both animal and vegetable life; in other words, that the compound called protoplasm is common to both. We have reason to believe that such is not the case, however. The essential difference between the three kingdoms of Nature lies in their spiritual origin and uses, and it is reasonable to suppose that a corresponding difference exists in the physical basis upon which each rests. We have called the structural element of the material kingdom the ethereal atom. That of the vegetable kingdom is termed protoplasm, likewise that of the animal kingdom. Yet the protoplasmic cell of the animal is not identical with that of the plant, for reasons above stated, and it remains for science to point out the exact distinction between them. Thus, the three kingdoms of Nature, reduced to their primary forms, are like three great planes which lie spread out indefinitely in all directions, but which never meet. The two lower are involved in the highest, but each remains distinct. No mineral ever becomes a plant, no plant ever becomes an animal. The lower of these forms are constantly becoming incorporated into the higher, but a *transubstantiation* is impossible. Thus, growth and development are limited in each of the divisions of Nature to its own domain respectively.

No one raises itself to a higher; there can be no progress of this sort. On the contrary, as surely as water runs down hill or a stone falls to the earth, so surely do all the forms of matter gravitate by a universal law toward a common level, that of their original elements. It is spiritual force alone, emanating from its supreme source, that restrains this tendency to dissolution.

Again, do the different genera and species of animals and plants ever pass into each other? The advocates of the development theory claim that such is the case, and that the higher forms of living organism were gradually derived from the lower. The arguments in support of this theory are drawn chiefly from observations upon the effects of domestication upon animals and plants. Subjected to new and peculiar conditions many animals and plants display marked variation from their original type. From this it has been inferred that by slow and gradual processes of nature, conducted through immense periods of time, these changes from the original type might result in new varieties and species. The truth is, the *first step* in this supposed development never takes place. There is no instance of a change of one species of animals into another within the memory of living men, nor do the history of past times or the records of geology bear witness to a single example of such a transformation. As, however, all things in the animal and vegetable kingdoms have relation to man, man being the sum of all created things, so that the "universe is but a larger body for his soul," we see in all forms, even the lowest, some representation of man. There is a *tendency* toward man in them all, as all are destined ultimately to be of use to him, and to become a part of him.

This is seen imperfectly in the mineral kingdom, in a more marked degree in the vegetable kingdom, and most of all in some of the higher and more perfect animals. Each is typical or prophetic of something higher. But such resemblances do not prove that man is in any sense a *result* of any of these lower forms by some process of differentiation or selection, however gradual. The weight of evidence goes to establish this truth, that a distinct germ is provided for every variety of animal and vegetable, and that no germ of one kind ever produces that of another. This germ is but a form or receptacle into which flows the peculiar spiritual force or life which is to characterize it and give it individuality. This gives to each particular member of a species its proper rank and prominence.

How is this argument, drawn from the effects of domestication upon animals, to be met? The answer is this: All improvement in the breeds of animals effected by the intervention of an intelligent human will, and whatever of native ferocity domestic animals have lost, and whatever of gentleness, docility, and intelligence they have gained, may safely be ascribed to the humanizing influence of their association with men. Moreover, these improvements are not permanent. Restore any of the domestic animals to their primitive surroundings and conditions, and they speedily relapse into their original savage state.

Were the cynic philosopher of Athens to come in our day with his lantern to search for man in the being constructed by a purely material science, by means of this process of development or natural selection, he would not find him. In reality, such theories as those of Darwin, Huxley, and their followers stop short of man altogether. They, at the most, predicate something of the body he dwells in. But the animal organism which man inhabits is no more the man himself than the house in which he lives. The difference between him and the lower animals is not to be sought for in physical conformation. His body is the highest form of organized matter, and it is so that his connection with the material world may be through the best possible medium. To accept such theories would be to deny that there is anything in man above nature. More than this, it would compel us to admit that all our acts are the result of co-ordinate natural forces operating through finely organized forms of matter; in a word, that man himself is the resultant of external circumstances, hereditary peculiarities, and acquired physical conditions. True, volition is allowed as a possible factor in his composition, but one having only a slight influence on the result. What is this *volition*, of which so little account is made? Is it not that immaterial part of man which clothes itself with the highest or primary forms of matter, and those confessedly, through which the intellectual operations are carried on, or the nerve tissue? In the progress of growth it is the *will* that determines the act, and actsdetermine structure, and so the man is builded. When by protracted mental effort I have wasted a certain portion of my brain tissue, and new matter has been appropriated to repair the waste, that portion of the brain has experienced an actual growth, and, after due rest, is capable of exerting a larger *effort* in the same direction; for the same law which obtains with muscle and sinew holds equally good with the brain. All physical activity is accompanied by a breaking down and waste of fiber in the parts employed in the action, the repair of which constitutes growth and development; and that marvelous hidden energy called *mind* destroys its covering of nerve tissue, but builds again larger and better, and it likewise directs and governs the growth of the whole body. It is thus that man's spirit reaches down into matter and gathers up its mantle of earth, which it shapes to itself, almost at will, and stamps its image on the plastic clay. Spirit acts upon matter, and not matter upon spirit. Thought and will are such spiritual agents. It is true that in man's more immediate relations with the world of matter there is a sort of mechanism, a reciprocity of impression and action, which affords an apparent basis for the theory we have endeavored to refute. The study of these mutual relations constitutes a legitimate branch of science, but it is only on a material plane that its investigations may be pursued, as no higher is admitted by those who cultivate it. They have no right to push their conclusions into a field belonging to a higher and truer science.

In the study of the natural sciences we recognize two classes of minds, one in its way as important as the other. There are those whose genius is of a narrow order, permitting them only to seize upon some few of the combinations of the great whole. They disregard the sum total in order to scrutinize details, because these they can subject to the analysis of reason, defining and limiting them, but unable to perceive their full and entire relations. There are grander minds whose broad range and comprehensive grasp can mass together and co-ordinate these isolated facts, fitting them into a connected series, deducing from them truths of highest import. These last catch glimpses of the true order of Nature. And there is a Supreme Intelligence, to whose clear, illimitable vision all things, both grandest and least, are in perfect harmonious order. Is unaided science able to arrive at a knowledge of this true order of Nature? No. Our Jacob's ladder must first be let down from heaven before we can climb its heights. It is impossible for the " natural to act upon the spiritual." We shall never reach heaven by any tower of Babel, however broadly we place the foundations, or however skillfully we lay the stones. Every object which pictures itself in the eye presents an inverted image on the retina. It is a heaven-born faculty alone that gives us erect vision. So the eye of science sees all things upside down, unless a spiritual insight is given to restore the true order. Science may pick out the letters, revelation alone can construct the word. How futile are our attempts to discover the origin and principles of things by purely scientific means. The microscopist peers into the inmost recesses of matter, and that which resists his last analysis is a nucleated cell, the particles of which are in rapid motion. The astronomer directs his most powerful lenses along the highways of space, and that which bounds his remotest vision is a nebulous mass, with a denser nucleus near its center, the egg, perhaps, of a universe, the minute star points of which are also in motion. In both directions infinity bounds the view. With the telescope we place ourselves at a distance, and get, as it were, a perspective view of creation. With the microscope we multiply infinity around us. We are no nearer the world of causes than before.

In the new theology, known as the New Jerusalem, now descending among men, is contained in its grand outlines the true system of the universe. The general plan is here; it remains for science to fill up the details. The wonderful scientific discoveries of the present day, rendered possible, we believe, by an antecedent influx of spiritual truth into the world, not only harmonize

in a striking manner with this general plan, but they also illus-
trate and confirm the system of theology which embodies it.   The
inspired teachings of the New Church enfold the broad and general principles that govern the order of Nature.   They teach that
which science now readily admits and confirms with abundant proofs
after twenty centuries of patient investigation—the unity of force !
It is in fact the ultimation of the unity of idea and singleness of
purpose of a One, Divine, and Personal Creator.   It has been our
humble effort to trace this force back to its source, to show that all
force, whether operating in the lowest crystal or in man, is spiritual; and this should be a cardinal doctrine of the New Science, as
it is of the New Theology.

The New Church University.

INAUGURAL ADDRESS,

Delivered at Commencement at Urbana University, June 7, 1871,

By the Rev. FRANK SEWALL, A. M., President.

Use is the law that governs the growth and determines the final success of institutions. Institutions that are not needed are sure to fail in the end, however they may be for a season held up and made to look prosperous by the selfish interest and devotion which founded them; but institutions whose foundations lie in the use they perform, or are laboring more and more effectually to perform in the community, are in the orderly, because in the heavenly way of growth and prosperity.

It is of great importance, therefore, that in inaugurating any new enterprise, a definite understanding be had of the especial use which this is to serve. For, if the labor be directed toward the particular use as an end, it may be done in reasonable hope of success; but whatever the end be, abstractly viewed, or not definitely viewed, or not definitely seen and practically labored for, the effort, directed by mere temporary expediency with shifting purpose and uncertainty of aim, will at length fail from sheer want of a proper understanding of its own use and of persistency in striving to fulfill it.

The question is asked, what is the use of more universities or colleges? And the question is well put as applying to such an institution as our own. It will not be inappropriate on the present occasion to say a few words in answer to this question, for it is a point which, on the grounds stated above, should be carefully considered by all who have the interests of our institution at heart.

It is really and practically of more importance to our ultimate success, to consider what is the peculiar use and end of our institution, than to consider how may we the most profitably sustain it pecuniarily for one, two, or a longer period of years.

Why multiply the colleges or institutions claiming that title, already so numerous in our land? In our own State of Ohio, there are no less than thirty institutions bearing the once honored and significant name of college or university. Besides the usually well-appointed high schools in all our cities and county towns, there is in almost every town or city of much importance a so-called college or university, more or less liberally endowed and numerously attended. What is the use of so many? Is it a numerical want? Is Urbana University needed because the accommodation is too scanty elsewhere, because there are not schools enough, or teachers enough, or buildings enough in proportion to the number of students applying? Surely this is not the case. Numerically considered, it were well if we had far fewer rather than a greater number of colleges, and if the few were filled to their capacity rather than leading a labored and impoverished existence, owing to thin attendance and scanty funds.

But the answer is usually made in defense of the multiplication of colleges so far beyond the numerical demand: "The want and the use is a denominational one; a want which, from the nature of our religious institutions as a people, can not be met in any other way than the establishment of special denominational colleges and seminaries."

The defense is a valid one, as generally employed. Whatever we may think of the importance or non-importance of the grounds of difference which divide and distinguish the Christian sects, it remains a fact, that while men remain as they are such differences will exist, and in the minds of those concerned will assume such an importance as to make the demand for denominational schools, and accordingly for denominational colleges, an imperative one. And no one would willingly see the freedom of such bodies in carrying out their ends infringed upon.

But reasonable as is this plea for denominational colleges, and the defense rested thereon for the otherwise unnecessary multiplication of schools of so high rank, is this our plea and our defense?

Is the use of Urbana University that of a denominational school and only that?

By a denominational school, I understand a school where the usual sciences are taught in the usual manner, but where, in what appertains to religion, the pupils are brought under the particular guidance and training of the respective denomination in whose interests the school is maintained. Thus the diversity of such schools and their distinctive character does not lie, at least to any essential degree, in any difference of scientific or literary instruction, but in those features which are held quite aloof from science and learning, namely, those appertaining to faith and religion.

A New Church school intended to furnish instruction in the usual branches to all who apply, and to bring its pupils under the religious influence and teachings of its doctrines and worship, is, in so far, a denominational school in precisely the sense of other similar institutions. A New Church college has this use to subserve, as at least one of its uses: to afford a place of literary, social, and religious training to young people from localities where privileges of this kind, in the New Church, do not exist. The parent may not be particular; he will hardly inquire what course of text-books, what kind of science or letters is taught; but he will, in sending his child away to be educated, consider whether to send him where he will be under New Church influences or under those of a religious body with whom he is not in the same sympathy. The schools being equal in all purely scientific respects, the New Churchman wants a New Church school, in order that while his child is being educated in letters, he may also be growing up in the faith and religious attachments of the New Church.

Such is the denominational plea for a New Church school. It is reasonable as far as it goes, but applies more properly to the primary and grammar school than to the college or university. For it is during the years of youth and the earlier training in school, that the pupil needs the surrounding influences and teachings which shall go to form his religious belief and character. The young man ready to enter college, and certainly the mature student ready to enter upon any of the higher professional courses of university study, will have his mind already fixed in the principles of his faith and of his conduct. For this reason many intelligent New Churchmen have questioned whether a higher school be needed for the New Church student who, already, in his earlier years, principled in the faith and life of the Church, should be capable of going forth into all fields of learning, to reap with profit, unhindered by denominational lines.

But beyond this mere denominational use of throwing about the pupil the religious influences of the Church, I maintain that the New Church University has a distinct and important use to perform, which is all its own, which no other institution can perform, and which justifies, therefore, abundantly the effort, which has here been inaugurated, of building up such an institution.

This distinctive use of the New Church University, a use distinct from that of a mere denominational New Church school, is to bring the light of the New Dispensation down into the realm of nature and of science itself. It is not to teach theology and religion alone and apart, and science and philosophy alone and apart, but to unite the two hitherto separated and irreconcilable factors into the sublime unity, order, and beauty in which they stand revealed in the light of the science of Correspondences and of the spiritual sense of the Scriptures. The Christian Church has taught religion through the pulpit for centuries, while in the lecture room science and philosophy have still taught pantheism, atheism, or deism, indifferent utterly to the voice of revelation. But we are come to another and new age—yea, and a new world !

The science of Correspondences, which teaches the law of the relation of natural to spiritual things and the doctrine of Discrete Degrees, throws a light upon all the realm of natural science, yea, assists the reason itself as with a new faculty, enabling not simply the believing but also the rational mind to see the unity of the universe, spiritual and natural, and the oneness of the God of nature with the God of the Christian revelation.

To bring thus the light of heaven to bear upon questions of earthly science, of human history and development, is an office compatible with only those higher pursuits of study which belong to the college or university. The youth at school is occupied with learning objects and effects; he is not yet ready to enter into the region of causes which are interior and further removed from nature; least of all, can he enter into the Divine ends of things; but with a mind well stored with the outward principles, forms, and rules of science, he is to be led in the college to an understanding of interior principles, or to learn more of the soul of things, and thence upward in the higher university course and in the vast field of the New Church Theology to pierce to a vision of final ends, or the purposes and methods, so far as they are revealed, of the Divine wisdom and the Divine love.

If this be the true end of a New Church University, have I exaggerated its worth in saying it has a use all its own, which no other institution can subserve, and which justifies abundantly our efforts; yea, which should encourage and animate us with hopeful confidence in the midst of whatever outward difficulties, and a general misapprehension of our aim?

And if this is our distinctive use—the one thing that gives us a moral right to exist, in view of the already existing superfluity of colleges in our land—then ought we not to have a single eye to the performance of this use, if we wish to permanently prosper? Our efforts, at the best, can be but feeble, and our talents miserably inadequate to so grand an ideal; but if it is the best we can afford, and the utmost of our honest ability, we may rest assured that with the use of what we have, our ability will increase. But it is all important that we keep our true end in view. If we lose sight of this, we shall find ourselves only unrightful and idle sup-planters of others who could much better fill our place. As a mere local day school, we would be competing without any suffi-cient warrant with the public or other schools which already abound. If, then, our New Church school must be something more, what shall it be? A school and a church, do you answer? But if this be all, why, then, not send our children into any town where there is a New Church pastor and congregation, and let them attend the public schools which are so ably appointed and well conducted? We find but small ground to justify any large expenditure for a denominational New Church school, if its use as a school be only that of any of the ordinary public or private day schools! Our school, like many others, may indeed be supported, or half supported, from a kind of local accident, while yet, for all the purposes of sound moral and literary education, it may far bet-ter have never existed at all. But if we bend all our efforts toward the performing of our peculiar use, the establishing of a New Church college, that is, of a school wherein the distinctive principles of the New Church shall come down even into the teachings of science itself, and if we make all other efforts subordinate to this ruling one, then we are justified in extending our influence as a school as widely as possible, and in striking down as well as upward, and in bringing as many grades and departments of teaching into our limits as we can consistently with our obliga-tions to our main and ruling purpose.

The world is ripe for an enterprise such as I have described. Science is ready to become the seer now that Faith no longer fears to reason. The teachers are abroad; their words fall frag-mentarily, but with a wondrous harmony and unity, upon a world listening for the New Faith and for the New Church. Somewhere, perhaps not in our day, nor even in our own clime, it shall be realized, when pupils and teachers shall be gathered together for the noble and delightful study of the Science of Nature in the light of the Word of God, in a New Church university.

PROSPECTUS AND CATALOGUE

OF

URBANA UNIVERSITY.

1871.

URBANA, O., June, 1871.

Trustees.

CALENDAR.

1871.—September 4, Monday..........Examination for Classes in the Grammar School.

September 5, Tuesday..........Examination for admission to Freshman Class.

December 1, Friday ....First Term ends.

December 4, Monday..........Second Term begins.

December 23, Saturday........Christmas Recess.

1872.—January 2, Tuesday.............Studies resumed.

March 1, Friday.................Second Term ends.

March 4, Monday................Third Term begins.

March 8, Friday.................Spring Exhibition.

March 29, Friday...............Easter Recess.

April 2, Tuesday................Studies resumed.

May 31, Friday..............⎱ Annual Examinations.
June 3, Monday..............⎰

June 4, Tuesday.................Awards and Closing Services in Chapel.

June 4, Tuesday.................Annual Meeting of the Board of Trustees.

June 5, Wednesday.............Commencement.

FACULTY.

The Rev. FRANK SEWALL, A. M., *President,*
Professor of Mental and Moral Science.

THOMAS F. MOSES, A. M., M. D.,
Professor of Natural Science.

HJALMAR H. BOYESEN, *Cand. Phil. Univ. of Norway,*
Instructor in the Greek and Latin Languages.

———— ————,
Preceptress of the Girls' School and of the Primary Department.

MRS. M. A. PURINTON,
Matron of the College Hall.

Urbana University.

This institution was established in the year 1850, at Urbana, in the State of Ohio, under a charter granted by the legislature of that State.

Founded in the interests of the New Church, and conducted under its auspices, it has for its object the education of youth in the useful arts and sciences, and in the true Christian religion. The controlling aim in its government and instruction is to combine with thorough scientific and literary culture a knowledge of the uses and duties of the Christian life, and to pursue the study of natural science and the development of the reason upon the principle of the entire and perfect harmony of these with revealed religion and the Word of God.

The institution is under the management of twelve trustees, who are required by the terms of the charter to be members of the New Church, or attached to the principles thereof. These trustees are divided into six classes which expire in annual succession, and the vacancies thus caused are filled by the remaining trustees.

The name of University was conferred by the State before any schools existed to form such an institution, the charter authorizing "an institution designed to encourage and promote the diffusion of knowledge in all the branches of academic, scientific, and exegetic instruction." An elementary school and preparatory or grammar school were first organized, and in the year 1853, with an efficient corps of professors in the three academic departments of language, the natural and the moral sciences, the College was fairly inaugurated. The first class was graduated in the degree of Bachelor of Arts in the year 1857, and for four successive years, classes were graduated in this degree. The outbreak of the war in 1861, combined with other adverse circumstances to render a suspension of the collegiate department necessary, and only the lower schools have since that time been sustained until the last year, when, with the election of the present President, the College organization was restored, and preparation was at once begun for re-establishing the College as soon as a class of students should be got together who had attained to the requisite standard for entering upon the Freshman year. A class of young men in the University Grammar School have been during the year actively preparing to enter upon the College course next September, and this, together with indications from abroad, leads the government to expect an auspicious inauguration of the College department with the Fall Term of the present year. Students entering in advanced standing will also be enabled to pursue their studies in the proper grade.

ADMISSION.

The standard for admission will be found in the Courses of Study given in the following pages. Students will be examined and assigned to their grades in the College or preparatory course, according to their attainments. They must furnish satisfactory evidence of a good moral character, and on entering the University, will be regarded as assuming the obligations of a strictly honorable and conscientious behavior. As soon as it becomes known that a student is deriving no benefit from his attendance, or that he persists in a course injurious to himself or his fellow students, his connection with the University will be promptly dissolved.

RELIGIOUS DUTIES.

The President assumes the pastoral charge of the University and attends to the religious education and doctrinal instruction of the students. Divine worship is held daily in the College, which the students and pupils are required to attend. Their attendance will also be required at the New Church service and Sunday-school on Sundays, except when excused for special reasons.

LOCATION.

The city of Urbana, in which the College is situated, is the county seat of Champaign county, and contains from four to five thousand inhabitants. The town is of a neat and tasteful character, with well-improved streets and pleasant gardens. The College grounds are in close proximity to the town and yet beyond the range of general habitation; they comprise thirty acres of native forest. Here are located the University Hall, containing the class rooms, library, etc., and the College Hall for the students' residence. Urbana is accessible by railroad from every direction. The express trains from New York, Philadelphia, Chicago, St. Louis, Cincinnati, and other important points stop here twice a day, affording the town unusual mail and traveling facilities.

PRICE OF TUITION.

The academic year of forty weeks is divided into three terms of thirteen weeks each, with a week's recess at Christmas.

The prices of tuition are:

In College (French, German, etc., included) ....$20 00 per term.
In Grammar School, according to grade, $12 to........ 15 00 " "
In Elementary School ,................................. 8 00 " "

French or German, extra in the schools.

BOARDING AND OTHER EXPENSES.

The price of board at the College Hall is $4.50 per week, washing, fuel, and lights not included. The rooms are plainly furnished, but the student is requested to bring with him, if convenient, a change of bed-linen and a strip of carpet two yards in length. The annual expenses may be roughly estimated thus:

Term Dues in College, at $20.00....................... $60 00
Boarding, 40 weeks, at $4.50......... .... 180 00
Washing, Fuel, Lights.................................... 40 00
Books, Library Fee, etc................................ 10 00

College students, or pupils of the grammar school, who, for the sake of economy, may desire to avail themselves of situations offered them in private families, or where boarding may be obtained at cheaper rates than at the College Hall, will be permitted to do so—said places having been first selected or approved by the College Faculty.

STUDIES—DEGREES.

THE COURSE IN ARTS.

The usual academic course of four years' study will be required of candidates for the degree of Bachelor of Arts. A careful and thorough training in the Greek and Latin languages will form an important feature of this course, and this not so much with a view to acquiring such knowledge as a literary accomplishment, as for the sake of the moral culture afforded by the familiar intercourse of the student's mind with the thoughts and customs of a past age, and also for that practical basis for the science of language, and thence for the science of thought itself, which the study of the ancient languages is peculiarly designed to supply. Far from being out of place in a scientific course, the study of the classics is regarded as itself strictly and in an eminent sense scientific, and as affording important elements of ethical and logical culture. The study of these languages, not as dead, but as living in the language and in the thought and affection of to-day, will give a breadth and depth to mental training worthy of the new age which is now first reducing the study of language to a science and the sciences themselves to their destined unity and harmony.

MODERN LANGUAGES.

Together with the study of Greek and Latin, careful attention will be paid to the practical acquirement of the modern European tongues, especially the French and German.

Conversational exercises, familiarizing the student with current idioms and familiar phrases in the spoken languages, will form an important feature of this branch, while due attention will be paid to the valuable fields of literature thus opened up to the student's research.

ENGLISH LANGUAGE—ANGLO-SAXON.

In literary study, no branch, however, will be regarded as more important than the study of our own English language, both in its present grammar and literature, and in its great Anglo-Saxon mother tongue. The study of Anglo-Saxon will form a distinct but regular feature of the course in Arts.

THE COURSE IN SCIENCE.

A three years' course of study largely occupied in the natural sciences and applied mathematics, and in which the Greek language is dispensed with, and only one college year's course of Latin required, will be requisite for the degree of Bachelor of Science. The higher mathematics, the familiar use of the French language, and a general survey of the natural and practical sciences, will be the chief characteristics of this course. Pupils in the Grammar School, who are not preparing for College, may substitute the modern languages for the classics, and take a *High School Course* in natural science, rhetoric, etc. But in the College, whether in the course in Arts or in Science, there will be no partial or special course allowed, nor other election of studies than such as is designated in the printed curriculum. Students of advanced grade, however, who can pass a satisfactory examination in studies pursued by them elsewhere, will be accredited with such in the assignment of their standing, and allowed to pursue exclusively those required branches in which they are deficient.

LECTURES—GENERAL EXERCISES.

During the present year the President has publicly delivered two courses of "UNIVERSITY LECTURES." The first, consisting of four lectures, was on the "Second Coming of the Lord as now being fulfilled;" the second, of six familiar lectures, on the "Internal Sense of the first Chapters of Genesis." Addressed especially to the members of the University, these lectures were listened to by a numerous general audience, including a number of the citizens of the town. Similar courses of lectures will form a regular feature of the educational course each year.

The immediate doctrinal instruction of the students and pupils is provided for in the Sunday-school under the direction of the President. The younger boys are required to learn the Lord's Prayer and the Ten Commandments, and the Universals of the Christian faith. The older students enter the doctrinal or Bible class and pursue regular studies in the Word, and also in some work selected from the writings of the Church as a text-book. The manual in use this year has been the "Doctrine of Life for the New Jerusalem.

In the day school an earnest effort has been made to promote a healthy and even development of the various faculties and tastes of the pupil's mind, by providing a series of weekly general exercises, illustrated lessons, and lectures, as follows:

IN DRAWING.—One hour a week for the whole school, from exercises in straight and curved lines to simple landscapes, architectural forms, and the human face.

IN MUSIC.—The rudiments of musical notation; reading at sight without instrumental accompaniment. In these exercises the whole school is engaged one hour a week. Opportunities are also provided for the training of all the students who desire it in the music of the church services, and for the formation of choral classes for the study of classical music.

ILLUSTRATED LECTURES IN GEOGRAPHY, POLITICAL and PHYSICAL.

LESSONS AND DRILLING EXERCISES IN ENGLISH.—Reading, Spelling, and Grammar.

ILLUSTRATED LECTURES IN ARCHITECTURE.

LIBRARY.

The libraries of the University comprise about 5,000 volumes, including a valuable complete set of the works of Swedenborg, both scientific and theological. A number of the leading literary magazines and the periodicals of the Church are received regularly at the library for the free use of the students.

DONATIONS, WANTS, ETC.

The University has the promise of several valuable donations of scientific books, mineralogical and other collections, on condition of the proper rooms being provided for their arrangement and preservation.

A liberal endowment is needed for completing the University Hall upon the original plan, providing a fire-proof library, lecture rooms, and chapel, and for the permanent maintenance of professorships in the several departments.

GENERAL PATRON.

As a precaution against extravagance, parents at a distance may deposit funds with the General Patron, who will, when requested, pay particular attention to the pecuniary concerns of the pupil or student, keeping a strict account with him, corresponding with the parent, and transmitting, at regular periods, an account of expenditures. The President will fulfill the duties of Patron the coming year.

THE SCHOOL FOR GIRLS.

At the recent annual meeting of the Board of Trustees, action was taken removing the girls' school, as also the primary classes, from the University Hall, and ordering the erection of a separate building for the girls' school and primary department as soon as practicable. Steps are already being taken to accomplish this, and it is not impossible that the building will be ready at the beginning of the Fall Term. Definite information can be obtained by inquiring of the Secretary of the Board, Mr. Milo G. Williams, Urbana.

NOTE.—Tuition fees must absolutely be paid in advance, and no student's or pupil's name will be placed on the roll except on presenting his term bill receipted, or else a special order from the Executive Committee of the Board permitting the enrollment of his name. Damages to the College property will be assessed on the perpetrator, or averaged on all the scholars when the perpetrator is unknown.

The library fee will be one dollar per year.

The Course of Study.

I. IN THE ELEMENTARY SCHOOL

Are taught Reading, Writing, Spelling, Arithmetic, Geography, Primary History of United States and England, Oral Grammar, and First Lessons in Composition; French (Mrs. Barbauld's First Lessons) and Latin at option.

II. THE UNIVERSITY GRAMMAR SCHOOL.

Standard Age of Entering, 14 Years.

FIRST YEAR.

FIRST TERM.

Latin—Harkness' Introductory Latin Book.
Arithmetic—Stoddard's Complete.
Geography—Guyot's Common School.
English—Reading, Spelling, Writing.

SECOND TERM.

Latin—Harkness' Latin Grammar.
Arithmetic—Continued.
Geography—Continued.
English—Reading, Spelling, and Letter Writing.

THIRD TERM.

Latin—Harkness' Latin Grammar and Allen's Reader.
Arithmetic—Continued.
Geography and History of the United States.
English—Written Exercises in Geography and History.

SECOND YEAR.

FIRST TERM.

Latin—Allen's Latin Reader; Latin Grammar.
Greek—Boise's First Greek Book, with Hadley's Grammar.
Mathematics—Stoddard's Arithmetic.
History—Anderson's General History, Ancient; Biblical Geography.

Latin—Allen's Reader ; Latin Grammar.
Greek—Grammar and First Lessons continued.
Mathematics—Loomis' Algebra.
History—Anderson, Medieval ; Classical Geography.

THIRD TERM.

Latin—Virgil's Æneid ; Prosody, Harkness' Grammar.
Greek—Xenophon's Anabasis, with Grammar.
Mathematics—Loomis' Algebra.
History—Anderson, Modern.
Physical Geography.

THIRD YEAR.

FIRST TERM.

Latin—Virgil's Æneid ; Arnold's Prose Composition.
Greek—Xenophon's Anabasis.
Mathematics—Loomis' Geometry, Four Books.
English—Grammar ; Parsing and Analysis.
History—Greek and Roman Antiquities, Bojesen's.

SECOND TERM.

Latin—Virgil's, Bucolics and Georgics ; Latin Prose Composition ; Cicero's Orations, Chase and Stewart's Selections.
Greek—The Iliad of Homer ; Greek Prose Composition.
Mathematics—Review of the Course.
English—Shaw's Specimens of English Literature.
History—Greek and Roman Antiquities, Bojesen's.

THIRD TERM.

Latin—Cicero's Orations ; Latin Prose Composition.
Greek—The Iliad of Homer ; Greek Prose Composition.
English—Hudson's School Shakespeare ; Reading and Parsing.
History—Selections from Medieval and Modern History, Putz and Arnold ; Hume Abridged.

III. THE HIGH SCHOOL COURSE.

This course comprises the Grammar School Course of three years, and adds thereto a fourth year course, allowing the substitution of the modern for the ancient foreign languages, and providing for the following additional studies :

Rhetoric—Quackenbos' Rhetoric and Composition.
Natural Philosophy—Rolfe and Gillet.
Chemistry—Rolfe and Gillet.
Mathematics, Trigonometry, and Surveying.
Astronomy—Hand-book of the Stars.
Geology and Mineralogy—Hitchcock.
Botany—Gray.
Anatomy and Physiology.
Divine Love and Wisdom—Swedenborg.
Religious System—Le Boys des Guays.
Science of Government—Alden.
Book Keeping and Letter Writing.

THE COURSE IN FRENCH.

Mrs. Barbauld's Lessons (Elementary) ; Otto's French Grammar ; Paul e Virginie ; Picciola ; Corinne ; Collot's Dramatie Reader ; Charles XII. ; Richer's Religion du bon Sens ; Letters á un Homme du Monde, Des Guay's ; Select Readings and Conversation.

THE COURSE IN GERMAN.

Otto's German Grammar ; Comfort's German Reader ; Auerbach's Dorfgeschichte ; Schiller's Wilhelm Tell ; Writing ; Conversation ; Goethe's Faust ; Lessing's Nathan der Weise.

THE COURSE IN DRAWING.

Lines straight and curved ; Geometrical Forms ; Solids ; Simple Landscape ; Architectural Forms ; Outlines of Flowers ; Outlines of Animals ; the Human Face ; the Human Form ; Architectural Design ; Mechanical Drawing.

THE COURSE OF RELIGIOUS INSTRUCTION.

The Word ; Bible History and Geography ; the Decalogue explained ; the Correspondence of Heat and Light ; Worcester's "Scripture Lessons ; " Reed's "Growth of the Mind ; " "The Doctrine of Life," "Of the Sacred Scripture," "Of the Lord," "Of Heaven and Hell," and the "True Christian Religion," by Swedenborg.

IV. THE COLLEGE.

TERMS OF ADMISSION.

Candidates for admission to the Freshman Class in the Academical Course will be examined in the following books and subjects:

Latin Grammar; Latin Prose Composition; Sallust or Cæsar, or Allen's Latin Reader; Virgil's Æneid; Cicero's Orations.

Greek Grammar; Xenophon's Anabasis, or Goodwin's Greek Reader; Homer's Iliad.

Algebra, to equations of the second degree; Geometry, the first and third books of Davies' Legendre.

English Grammar.

Ancient and Modern Geography.

CURRICULUM

FOR THE DEGREE OF BACHELOR OF ARTS.

FRESHMAN YEAR.

LATIN.—Livy, two books; Horace—Odes, Satires, Epistles; Latin Prose Composition.

GREEK.—Xenophon's Memorabilia; Goodwin's Greek Moods and Tenses; Arnold's Greek Prose Composition; The Odessy of Homer; Herodotus.

MATHEMATICS.—Algebra; Geometry; Plane Trigonometry.

HISTORY.—Smith's Greece; Liddell's Rome.

FRENCH.—Otto's French Grammar; Collot's Reader; Guizot's Histoire de la Civilization.

SOPHOMORE YEAR.

LATIN. — Cicero — Tusculan Disputations; Tacitus — Histories, Germania and Agricola.

GREEK.—Demosthenes' Orations; The Prometheus of Eschylus; The New Testament.

MATHEMATICS.—Plane and Spherical Trigonometry; Navigation; Surveying; Analytical Geometry.

RHETORIC.—Quackenbos' Rhetoric and Composition.

HISTORY.—Schwegler's History of Philosophy; Authenticity of the Gospels, Chandler.

ENGLISH LANGUAGE.—Craik's English of Shakespeare; Marsh's Philological Method; Morris' Early English.

JUNIOR YEAR.

LATIN.—Juvenal; Terrence; De Divino Amore—Swedenborg.

MATHEMATICS.—Calculus; Astronomy.

NATURAL PHILOSOPHY.—Snell's Olmstead's.

CHEMISTRY.—Youman's.

HISTORY.—The Student's Gibbon's Rome.

NATURAL HISTORY.—Ware.

RHETORIC AND LOGIC.—Themes; Discussions; Trench on the Study of Words.

GERMAN LANGUAGE.—Otto's Grammar; Goethe's Faust; Lessing's Nathan der Weise.

OPTIONAL.—*Greek.*—Plato's Gorgias; Sophocles' Antigone; The New Testament.

SENIOR YEAR.

DE DIVINA PROVIDENTIA.—Swedenborg.

NATURAL SCIENCE.—Geology and Mineralogy; Zoology; Anatomy and Physiology; Botany.

ANGLO SAXON.—March; Thorpe's Analecta Anglo-Saxonica.

HISTORY.—Putz and Arnold's Modern History.

POLITICAL ECONOMY.—Alden's Science of Government; Hallam's Middle Ages; United States Constitution.

PHYSICS.—La Physique Moderne—Saigey.

THE SCIENCE OF CORRESPONDENCES.—Swedenborg—"Des Representations et des Correspondences;" The Divine Attributes.

RHETORIC.—Forensics and Themes, monthly; Reading and Oratory.

OPTIONAL.—*Latin.*—Quintillian; Pliny; Lucretius; Augustine's "Confessions," or "De Civitate Dei."

Greek.—The Republic of Plato; Thucydides; Plutarch.

Italian.—Grammar; Pellico's Mei Prigione; Dante.

German.—Goethe's Italianische Briefe; Lessing's Laocoon; Schiller's Don Carlos.

REVIEW AND EXAMINATION FOR DEGREE OF BACHELOR OF ARTS.

CURRICULUM

FOR THE DEGREE OF BACHELOR OF SCIENCE.

This is a Three Years' Course, requiring for admission the same which is required for the Academical Course, with the exception of the Greek language.

THE FIRST YEAR.

The same as the course of the Freshman Year excepting the Greek, for which is substituted Physical Geography and Ganot's Physics.

THE SECOND YEAR.

MATHEMATICS.—Plane and Spherical Trigonometry; Analytical Geometry; Calculus; Kerr's Mechanics; Navigation; Surveying.

CHEMISTRY.—Youman's New Chemistry.

MINERALOGY AND GEOLOGY.—Dana.

METALLURGY AND MINING.

DRAWING.—Mechanical and Topographical.

FRENCH.—Des Guay's Lettres; La Physique Moderne—Saigey.

THE THIRD YEAR.

THE STUDY OF DEGREES AND OF CORRESPONDENCE.—Swedenborg on the Divine Love and Wisdom; Divine Attributes; Principia; On the Infinite.

ANATOMY AND PHYSIOLOGY.—Draper.

ZOOLOGY.—Agassiz.

AGRICULTURAL CHEMISTRY; BOTANY.

ASTRONOMY.

ENGLISH LANGUAGE.—Morris' Specimens; March's Method.

GERMAN LANGUAGE. [Optional.]

HISTORY OF THE ARTS AND OF COMMERCE..

DRAWING.—Architectural; Linear Perspective.

REVIEW AND EXAMINATION FOR THE DEGREE OF BACHELOR OF SCIENCE.

REGISTER OF PUPILS
1 8 7 0 - 1.

ELEMENTARY SCHOOL.

Preceptress..*MISS F. P. BARNES.*

Boys.
ALBRIGHT, CLARENCE .... Urbana, O.
CANDY, THOMAS .... " "
GANSON, JONAS R. .... " "
HILL, FRANK.. " "
HUSTON, RICHARD.. " "

Girls.
FISLER, ANNIE .... Urbana, O.
GANSON, EMMA .... " "
HUSTON, ELLA.. " "
HUSTON, SALLIE... " "
NILES, GERTRUDE .... " "
OWEN, EFFIE... " "
RUGAR, CORABELLE BEERS .... Galesburg, Ill.
SMITH, JESSE.. Urbana, O.

GRAMMAR SCHOOL.
Boys.
BAILLIE, WILLIAM S. .... Urbana, O.
BOYESEN, INGOLF K. .... Kongsberg, Norway.
BOYESEN, ALF E. .... " "
BRYAN, LEVI.. Mad River Tp., Ch. Co., O.
CLARKE, WILLIAM .... Urbana, O.
DUNAYSKI, FRANZ... Dantzig, Prussia.
DYER, CHARLES L. .... New York City.
ESPY, JOSIAH H. .... Urbana, O.
FITHIAN, WILLIAM .... " "
GRIST, JOEL C. .... Morris, Ill.
GRANGER, HOLLIS RALPH .... Mobile, Ala.
HAY, HENRY CLINTON... Portland, Me.
HORR, OBED... Urbana, O.
MATTHIAS, CHARLES... Pittsburg, Pa.
NILES, ROBERT.. New York City.
RICHARDSON, WILLIAM C. .... St. Louis, Mo.
ROBERTS, WILLIAM B. .... Glendale, O.
SCHARLACH, FERNANDO L. L. .... Chicago, Ill.
SHOWERS, FRANK .... Urbana, O.
SMITH, MILLARD F. .... " "
SOWLES, FRANK VAME... " "
WHEELWRIGHT, FRANK .... " "
WHEELWRIGHT, HARRY... " "

GIRLS.

COULTER, MARY L. .... Columbus, O.
ESPY, CLARA.. Urbana, O.
FISLER, LILLIE...   "   "
FULTON, ELLA ....   "   "
HORR, WINNIE G. ....   "   "
KEATS, ALICE...... ....   "   "
MARSHALL, EVA............................. ....   "   "
RING, ELIZABETH C. ....   "   "
RUGAR, JANE SHEPPARD.................................... Galesburg, Ill.
SMITH, ADDIE .... Urbana, O.
TIPTON, LILLIE A. .... Griggsville, Ill.
WHEELWRIGHT, MARY B. .... Urbana, O.

COLLEGE CLASS.

PREPARING TO ENTER AT THE FALL TERM, 1871,

For the Degree, A. B.

BOYESEN, INGOLF KROG................... .... Kongsberg, Norway.
DYER, CHARLES L. .... New York City.
HAY, HENRY CLINTON....................... .... Portland, Me.
MATTHIAS, CHARLES .... Pittsburg, Pa.
ROBERTS, WILLIAM B. .... Glendale, O.
SCHARLACH, FERNANDO L. L. .... Chicago, Ill.
SOWLES, FRANK VAME.................................... Urbana, O.

For the Degree, S. B.

GRIST, JOEL C. .... Morris, Ill.